Customer Service Excellence:

A Guide to Winning

and Keeping Customers

First Published 2024

Customer Service Excellence

ISBN: 9798328793049

Copyright © 2024 Derek Good

Customer Service:

"Customer service refers to the assistance and support provided by a business to its customers before, during, and after a purchase or transaction."

Customer Service Excellence:

"Customer service excellence refers to consistently exceeding customer expectations and delivering exceptional service at every touchpoint throughout the customer journey."

Contents

Foreword by Paul Linnell

These are very challenging times for customer service.

A perfect storm has developed where significant advances in technology are making many customer interactions open to automation, and many organisations are embracing multi-channel engagement strategies. At the same time, the world is under pressure from financial uncertainties, global unrest and the pressures from a need for sustainability.

This is tempting many organisations to devise "cost-saving" customer interaction strategies that exploit inappropriate or unready technology and force customers to interact with them at times, through channels and at the convenience to the organisation, instead of times, channels, and at the convenience of their customers. For many, this is resulting in a reduced investment in customer service resources, less training, less accountability, and indeed, less "excellence".

And so, Derek's book **"Customer Service Excellence"** steps-in with a perfectly well-timed and important message that the real success of an organisation isn't achieved by delivering its products and services to customers at the lowest cost, it's achieved by delivering products and services for which their customers receive the highest value.

In these pages Derek reminds us that the importance of good customer service is as old as trade itself, and that success comes from making it easier for customers to do business **with us**, than with **our competitors**. Drawing on his decades of experience advising, training and coaching organisations in multiple industries in **customer excellence**, Derek has packed this book with tools, tips and techniques to help us all **deliver it**.

Paul Linnell: (Founder of CTMA and creator of the CTMA Customer-Driven Framework for Continuous Improvement, Innovation and Value Creation)

A Brief History of Customer Service

Customer Service is a concept that has been around a long time. Although people have a different view on what customer service is, it's possible to see its existence in ancient civilizations, such as Mesopotamia and Egypt. Some rudimentary forms of customer service emerged alongside early trade and barter systems. Merchants interacted directly with customers, providing goods and services in exchange for payment or goods of equivalent value.

Then, during the Middle Ages, guilds played a significant role in regulating trade and ensuring quality craftsmanship. Guild members were expected to uphold certain standards of service and craftsmanship, fostering trust and accountability among customers.

The Industrial Revolution brought about significant changes in customer service practices as mass production and urbanization transformed economies. With the rise of factories and large-scale manufacturing, businesses began to prioritise efficiency and standardised processes, often at the expense of personalised customer interactions.

In the late 19th and early 20th centuries, the emergence of department stores revolutionised retailing and customer service. Retail pioneers like Marshall Field and John Wanamaker introduced innovative practices such as fixed pricing, money-back guarantees, and courteous service, setting new standards for customer experience.

The invention of the telephone and the rise of mail-order catalogue companies, such as Sears, Roebuck and Co., further transformed customer service in the early 20th century. Businesses began to leverage these communication channels to interact with customers remotely, expanding their reach and enhancing convenience.

The post-World War II era saw a proliferation of consumer culture and the rise of service-oriented industries, such as banking, insurance, and hospitality. Companies increasingly prioritised customer satisfaction and loyalty, recognising the importance of delivering exceptional service to gain a competitive edge.

The advent of the internet and digital technologies in the late 20th and early 21st centuries revolutionized customer service once again. E-commerce platforms enabled businesses to engage with customers online, offering convenience, personalised recommendations, and 24/7 support.

One error some companies made in the internet boom was to try and get all their customers to go to websites. This of course alienated those that didn't have the internet or preferred more traditional channels. Companies had to quickly change their approach and offer multiple channels of customer interaction and make it about the customer's preference rather than a company centric approach.

Today is about the Omnichannel Customer Experience. Customer service encompasses a wide range of channels, including phone, email, live chat, social media, and mobile apps. Businesses strive to deliver seamless, omnichannel experiences that meet the evolving expectations of customers in an increasingly digital world.

Throughout history, customer service has evolved in response to changing economic, technological, and societal factors. From early trade and craftsmanship to the digital age of e-commerce and omnichannel support, the fundamental goal remains the same: to provide exceptional service and build lasting relationships with customers.

Customer Service Excellence

So what is customer service? In a nutshell, it's the support and assistance given to a customer before, during and after the provision of products or services. It includes a range of activities that are aimed at providing a level of satisfaction to the customer and generating loyalty from the customer. We will discuss a number of those activities throughout this book but for now, let's look at how we might define a bit more closely what customer service is and in particular, what makes excellent customer service.

Is it good customer service to get the correct answer but not the one you want? Or to be answered quickly but with the wrong answer? Or to be answered quickly with the right answer but be treated rudely? What is it that customers want and what is considered excellent service?

As a customer myself, I want to be treated with respect, as quickly as possible and be given the right information. That's good customer service. Excellent customer service is to get all of that and be given something a little extra – some added value – like a suggestion to help in the future. This could be a reference number in case I need to call back, an easier way to interact that may suit me – like an online portal, the best time or person to contact if I do need to contact them again or perhaps even some quick tips on how to use the product or service I am interested in or just purchased.

Everyone seems to be lacking in time these days, so to be dealt with in a timely manner is very important but we may all be willing to sacrifice a bit of time if we end up getting a satisfactory result. After all, there's no point being served fast if the result is wrong. So excellent customer service is the right combination of all those things: fast, reliable, correct, respectful service with some added value if possible.

Excellent customer service then goes beyond merely addressing the concern or need of the customer, it involves delivering a consistently exceptional experience that exceeds customer expectations, fosters trust, and builds lasting relationships.

Organisations that prioritise excellence in customer service tend to have a customer-centric approach which can often differentiate them from competitors. Even if the organisation isn't focused on this, an individual can make a massive impact by having a personal mission to provide a high level of service and can stand out from colleagues as well as create loyal customers through a consistent, personalised service which exceeds that experienced elsewhere.

Effective customer service is crucial for businesses as it can influence customer perceptions, brand reputation, and overall success. Companies that prioritise customer service often focus on training their employees, implementing efficient communication channels, and continuously improving their processes to meet or exceed customer expectations.

What you will find in this book are several key strategies and tips to help you avoid the mistakes that will turn customers away. You will see some repeated themes; things like active listening, showing empathy and anticipating future needs are worth highlighting more than once and you will see their emphasis as you read through the sections.

The Customer that Never Comes Back!

Samuel Moore Walton (March 29, 1918 – April 5, 1992) was an American business magnate best known for founding Walmart, shared these words of wisdom, "Believe me, customers never comes back!"

Years ago, Sam Walton opened a training program for its employees. When everyone was expecting a talk about sales and service, he started with these words:

"I'm the guy who goes to a restaurant, sits at the table and waits patiently, while the waiter does everything but write down my order." I'm the guy who goes to a store and waits quietly, while the salesmen finish their personal conversations. I'm the guy who walks into a gas station and never uses his horn, but patiently waits for the employee to finish reading his newspaper.

I'm the man who explains his desperate urgency for one piece but doesn't complain that he only gets it after three weeks of waiting.

I'm the guy that, when he enters a commercial establishment, seems to be asking for a favour, begging for a smile or just hoping to be noticed.

You must be thinking I'm a quiet, patient, never troublesome type... Get fooled.

Do you know who I am? I am the customer who never returns!
I love seeing millions spent annually on all sorts of ads to get me back to your company. Because when I first

went there, all they should have done was just a little, simple and inexpensive kindness: treat me with a little more courtesy.

There's only one boss: THE CUSTOMER. And he can fire everyone in the company from the president to the janitor, simply taking their money to spend elsewhere."

If you want to be successful, have better customer service than anyone else.

The Fish! Philosophy

The wonderful 'Fish! Philosophy' technique that was brought about by John Christensen following a visit to Pike Place Fish market in Seattle Washington in 1997 sums up four techniques that help to create a workplace culture that is infectious and great to be around. It provided an amazing place to visit for customers. The four basic tenets of the Fish! Philosophy are:

1. 'Being There'

2. 'Have Fun'

3. 'Choose your Attitude'

4. 'Make Their Day'.

During this book, we will be looking at these four areas in detail as they help to underpin the excellent customer service culture you can bring to your own organisation.

Internal customer service

Internal customer service refers to the support and assistance provided to fellow employees and other departments within an organisation to facilitate the smooth execution of tasks and achieve common goals. It involves viewing colleagues and other departments as valued customers and actively striving to meet their needs and exceed their expectations. By adopting a proactive and service-oriented mindset towards internal interactions, individuals can contribute to a positive work environment and enhance overall organisational effectiveness.

From an individual perspective, recognising fellow employees and other departments as internal customers is essential. By understanding that helping colleagues succeed in their roles ultimately benefits both the organisation and you, individuals can align their actions with the collective goals of the team. Embracing this perspective fosters a sense of collaboration and mutual support, laying the foundation for effective internal customer service.

Approaching opportunities to serve internal customers with positivity and enthusiasm is key to fostering a culture of internal customer service. Taking pride in one's ability to assist others and contribute to their success creates a virtuous cycle of reciprocity. When individuals demonstrate a willingness to go above and beyond to help their colleagues, they not only strengthen relationships within the organisation but also build trust and goodwill.

Exceeding internal customers' expectations is a hallmark of exceptional internal customer service. Just as individuals appreciate when their own expectations are exceeded, striving to delight internal customers with exceptional service sets a standard of excellence. By consistently delivering high-quality support and exceeding internal customers' expectations, individuals can cultivate a reputation for reliability and professionalism within the organisation.

Expressing gratitude is a simple yet powerful way to foster a culture of internal customer service. A genuine thank-you acknowledges the value of collaboration and reinforces a sense of appreciation among colleagues.

By expressing gratitude for assistance received and recognising the contributions of others, individuals can nurture an atmosphere of camaraderie and goodwill, where mutual support and cooperation thrive.

Internal customer service is integral to fostering a collaborative and productive work environment. By adopting a service-oriented mindset, exceeding internal customers' expectations, and expressing gratitude for support received, individuals can contribute to a culture of internal customer service that enhances organisational effectiveness and promotes collective success.

Proactive Customer Service

Proactive customer service is a positive approach that anticipates and addresses customer needs before they even realise they have them. By staying one step ahead of potential issues or concerns, businesses can impress their customers and enhance their overall experience. Here are a few ideas around the importance of proactive customer service and some practical strategies for implementation:

Anticipating Customer Needs: Proactive customer service involves anticipating what customers may need in the future, whether dealing with a specific issue or in general. By putting yourself in the customer's shoes, you can identify potential pain points and proactively address them before they escalate. For example, if a customer is calling about a delivery, provide them with a specific phone number or website address for tracking to streamline their experience.

Keeping Customers Informed: Keep customers informed about the status of their orders, deliveries, or any potential delays or issues. If you know something is behind schedule, proactively notify the customer and provide updates on the situation. Transparency and open communication demonstrate your commitment to customer satisfaction and build trust and loyalty.

Initiating Contact: Take the initiative to contact customers first if you identify any missing information or discrepancies in their orders or forms. Rather than waiting for the customer to follow up, reaching out proactively shows that you're proactive in resolving issues and reducing customer effort. By taking ownership of the situation and addressing concerns promptly, you can prevent potential frustrations and enhance the customer experience.

Reducing Customer Effort: Proactive customer service is ultimately about reducing the effort customers need to expend to resolve issues or obtain information. By anticipating their needs and providing relevant resources or assistance proactively, you can streamline the customer journey and make it easier for them to do business with you. This proactive approach not only enhances customer satisfaction but also increases loyalty and generates positive word-of-mouth referrals.

Increasing Customer Loyalty: By consistently delivering proactive customer service, businesses can increase customer loyalty and satisfaction. When customers feel valued and supported, they are more likely to remain loyal to your brand and recommend it to others. Proactive service demonstrates your commitment to customer success and sets you apart from competitors, fostering long-term relationships and driving business growth.

Proactive customer service is an approach that anticipates and exceeds customer needs, ultimately enhancing the overall customer experience. By engaging in these practices, businesses can differentiate themselves in a competitive market and build strong and lasting relationships with their customers..

Acknowledge Customer Contact

Have you ever walked into a store or contacted a business, only to feel like you're invisible? Have you sent an email to a company and wondered if it vanished into cyberspace? As customers, we all crave a sense of importance, acknowledgment, and being heard. It's essential for businesses to prioritise these aspects of customer interaction to nurture positive relationships and experiences.

Acknowledging every interaction with your customers is paramount. Whether it's through an email, a phone call, or a visit to your physical location, every contact point is an opportunity to make customers feel valued. For online inquiries, implementing an immediate auto-response to acknowledge receipt of their message can reassure customers that their communication hasn't gone unnoticed. Additionally, providing an estimated timeframe for when they can expect a personalised response adds transparency and demonstrates your commitment to addressing their needs promptly.

Similarly, in brick-and-mortar establishments, simple gestures like making eye contact, offering a warm greeting, and letting customers know you'll be available to assist them shortly can make a significant difference in their experience. A genuine smile and a friendly approach go a long way in conveying attentiveness and care.

It's crucial to extend this acknowledgment across all points of contact, whether it's interacting with customers over the phone, at the front desk, or during service visits. Each interaction is an opportunity to make customers feel valued and heard.

By simply acknowledging and actively engaging with customers at every touchpoint, businesses can create an environment where customers feel respected, appreciated, and more likely to return for future interactions. These small yet meaningful gestures contribute to building lasting relationships and growing customer loyalty.

The Power of Attitude

Your attitude counts

In the world of customer service, attitude is not just a part of the equation; it's the foundation upon which exceptional service is built. Picture this: you walk into a store greeted by a sales representative with a warm smile, genuine enthusiasm, and a willingness to assist you. Compare that with another scenario where you're met with indifference, a lacklustre attitude, and minimal effort to address your needs. Which experience leaves a lasting impression? Undoubtedly, the former.

Attitude shapes every interaction we have with customers. It's not just what we say or do, but how we convey it that truly matters. Here's why attitude is paramount in delivering customer service excellence:

First Impressions Count: As the saying goes, "You never get a second chance to make a first impression." The attitude we display in those initial moments sets the tone for the entire customer experience. A positive attitude instantly puts customers at ease, making them more receptive to our assistance and more likely to engage positively. More on a positive first impression later.

Empathy and Understanding: A positive attitude enables us to empathise with customers and understand their needs better. When customers feel understood and valued, they're more likely to trust our recommendations and remain loyal to our brand. Empathy fosters genuine connections, turning a transactional encounter into a meaningful interaction.

Problem-Solving Mindset: Inevitably, challenges arise in customer interactions. Whether it's a product issue, a billing discrepancy, or a service complaint, our attitude can make all the difference in resolving the issue satisfactorily. A proactive, solution-oriented attitude demonstrates our commitment to customer satisfaction and reinforces trust in our ability to address concerns effectively.

Building Rapport and Loyalty: Customers remember how we made them feel long after the interaction ends. A positive attitude creates memorable experiences that resonate with customers, fostering loyalty and prompting them to return. Moreover, satisfied customers are more likely to spread positive word-of-mouth recommendations, contributing to the growth and success of our business.

Personal Fulfilment: Beyond its impact on customers, cultivating a positive attitude brings personal fulfilment and job satisfaction. When we approach each interaction with enthusiasm, optimism, and a genuine desire to help, we not only elevate the customer experience but also derive greater joy and fulfilment from our work.

Consider that your attitude is the one true thing you have complete control over. Regardless of what is going on around you, you have the choice on how to react to it. If you really don't want to be at work, it will come through in your mannerisms. When you make a deliberate choice of how to be, you can change the outcome of any interaction.

Avoid blaming other people if things haven't been done or something has gone wrong. To the customer you are all one business organisation. They don't want to hear if it's the fault of purchasing or the courier – to them it's all the same. Avoid using blame as a way of dodging the customer's wrath. It's much better to own up to a problem and show you're willing to sort it out.

Attitude is contagious—it sets the tone for customer interactions and significantly influences the outcome. By embracing a positive attitude, we not only enhance the customer experience but also cultivate a culture of service excellence within our organisation. As you embark on this journey of delivering excellent customer service, remember that your attitude is your most potent tool—one that has the power to transform ordinary interactions into extraordinary experiences.

The Cost of Indifference

Neglecting customer concerns can harm your business. Even more frightening is how an attitude of indifference in any interaction can turn customers away without having to do anything majorly wrong. These days, competition is fierce and customer loyalty is paramount so knowing that indifference can be a silent killer can help you stay ahead. Defined as a lack of interest or concern, indifference towards customers can have far-reaching consequences, ultimately leading to loss of business and damage to reputation. We are going to look at the detrimental effects of indifference on customer interactions and explore strategies to overcome it.

Imagine this scenario: a customer reaches out to your business with a query or concern, seeking assistance or resolution. However, instead of receiving the attentive and empathetic response they expect, they are met with indifference. Perhaps the response lacks warmth, or worse, the customer feels dismissed or disregarded. In that moment, the seeds of dissatisfaction are sown, and the customer's perception of your business tarnished.

Studies show that one of the primary reasons customers defect to competitors is the feeling of being unappreciated or undervalued by their current provider. When customers sense indifference from a business, they are more inclined to seek alternatives where they feel their needs and concerns are acknowledged and addressed. The ripple effect of customer churn can be significant, as dissatisfied customers not only take their own business elsewhere but also influence others in their network to do the same.

But how can businesses combat indifference and cultivate a customer-centric approach? The key lies in making each customer feel special and valued. Here are some actionable strategies to overcome indifference in your role:

Personalise the Experience: Treat each customer interaction as an opportunity to build a genuine connection. Address them by name, and tailor your responses to their specific needs and circumstances. By acknowledging their individuality, you demonstrate that their concerns are important to you.

Practice Active Listening: Truly listen to what the customer is saying, without interruption or distraction. Pay attention not only to the words they speak but also to the emotions underlying their communication. Empathise with their situation and show genuine concern for their well-being.

Display Empathy: Put yourself in the customer's shoes and try to understand their perspective. Empathy involves recognising and validating the customer's feelings, whether they are frustrated, disappointed, or upset. By showing empathy, you can build trust and rapport with the customer.

Be Solution-Oriented: Instead of focusing on limitations or constraints, adopt a proactive approach to problem-solving. Explore creative solutions and alternatives to address the customer's needs effectively. Demonstrate a willingness to go above and beyond to help them achieve a satisfactory outcome.

Express Gratitude: Acknowledge the customer's loyalty and express gratitude for their business. A simple "thank you for choosing us" or "we appreciate your support" can go a long way in making the customer feel valued and appreciated.

Indifference towards customers is a dangerous pitfall that businesses must avoid at all costs. By prioritising customer satisfaction and cultivating a culture of empathy and engagement, businesses can foster long-term relationships with their customers and distinguish themselves in a competitive market. Remember, every customer interaction is an opportunity to leave a lasting impression and build brand loyalty. So, strive to overcome indifference and create memorable experiences for your customers, one interaction at a time.

Creating Moments of Delight

In any customer interaction, there exists a profound opportunity, to not just meet customers' needs but to exceed their expectations and make their day. Imagine the impact of turning an ordinary transaction into a memorable experience - one that leaves customers feeling valued, appreciated, and genuinely delighted.

Let's take a look at the art of making the customer's day – one of the four Fish! Philosophy tenets mentioned earlier - and the transformative power it holds in fostering lasting relationships and driving business success.

Surprise and Delight: A key strategy in making the customer's day is the element of surprise. By going above and beyond what is expected, we can pleasantly surprise customers and leave a lasting impression. Whether it's a handwritten thank-you note, a complimentary upgrade, or a small token of appreciation, these unexpected gestures elevate the customer experience and create moments of delight.

Personalisation: Tailoring our interactions to the individual preferences and needs of customers demonstrates that we see them as more than just transactions - we see them as unique individuals with distinct preferences and interests. Personalised recommendations, customised solutions, and remembering details about their past interactions enhance the sense of connection and make customers feel valued and understood.

Anticipating Needs: Proactively anticipating and addressing customers' needs before they even realise them showcases our commitment to their satisfaction and convenience. Whether it's offering assistance before they ask for it, providing relevant information proactively, or resolving potential issues pre-emptively, this proactive approach demonstrates our attentiveness and dedication to making their experience seamless and hassle-free.

Creating Emotional Connections: Beyond meeting functional needs, we have the opportunity to create emotional connections with customers. By showing empathy, actively listening to their concerns, and expressing genuine care and concern, we foster trust and loyalty that transcends the transactional aspect of the relationship. Emotional connections build long-term loyalty and turn satisfied customers into passionate advocates for our brand.

Going the Extra Mile: Sometimes, making the customer's day requires us to go the extra mile - whether it's staying late to assist a customer, resolving a complex issue with patience and dedication, or simply taking the time to chat and brighten their day. These acts of kindness and dedication leave a lasting impact and create loyal customers who return time and again.

Making the customer's day is not just about providing excellent service - it's about creating memorable experiences that leave a positive impression long after the interaction ends. By infusing every interaction with warmth, empathy, and a genuine desire to exceed expectations, you have the power to make a difference in the lives of your customers and elevate your service from ordinary to extraordinary. Consider what you can do to embrace the opportunity to make each customer's day a little brighter and your business a beacon of excellent service.

Being Present

In the customer service industry, being physically present is only half the battle. True excellence in service requires a deeper level of engagement - a mental presence that allows us to focus fully on the needs and experiences of our customers. Here are a few ideas that help highlight the importance of being mentally present in customer interactions and the deep impact it can have on delivering exceptional service.

Active Listening: Once again, this is fundamental in providing a great customer experience. Active listening is at the heart of being mentally present. This means not only hearing what the customer is saying but truly understanding their perspective, concerns, and underlying needs. By giving our full attention to the customer, we validate their importance and build trust, paving the way for more meaningful interactions.

Empathetic Understanding: Being mentally present enables us to empathise with customers on a deeper level. It allows us to step into their shoes, acknowledge their emotions, and respond with compassion and understanding. Empathy fosters genuine connections and demonstrates that we care about more than just completing a transaction - we care about their well-being and satisfaction.

Focusing on the Present Moment: In a world filled with distractions, being mentally present requires a conscious effort to focus on the here and now. By setting aside distractions such as phones, multitasking, or internal distractions, we can fully immerse ourselves in the customer interaction, giving them our undivided attention and making them feel valued and respected.

Cultivating Curiosity: A mentally present mindset encourages curiosity and a genuine interest in the customer's needs and preferences. By asking thoughtful questions, seeking to understand their unique circumstances, and exploring potential solutions together, we demonstrate our commitment to finding the best possible outcome for the customer.

Adaptability and Problem-Solving: Being mentally present enables us to adapt quickly to changing circumstances and think critically to solve problems effectively. Instead of being reactive or following scripted responses, we can approach each situation with creativity and flexibility, finding innovative solutions that meet the customer's needs and exceed their expectations.

Maintaining a Positive Attitude: Mental presence also involves maintaining a positive attitude, even in challenging situations. By approaching each interaction with optimism, resilience, and a can-do attitude, we inspire confidence in our ability to resolve issues and create positive outcomes for customers.

Being mentally present in customer interactions is essential for delivering exceptional service. It allows us to listen actively, empathise genuinely, and respond thoughtfully to the needs of our customers. By cultivating a mindset of mindfulness and engagement, we can create memorable experiences that leave a lasting impression and build long-term loyalty.

Harnessing the Power of Fun in Customer Service

In the pursuit of customer service excellence, one often overlooked ingredient is the power of fun. Creating a work environment where joy, enthusiasm, and camaraderie abound not only enhances employee satisfaction but also translates into remarkable experiences for customers. You can see the impact that having fun at work can have by elevating the customer service experience to a new level. Here are some ways to have fun at work:

Creating a Positive Atmosphere: Fun at work sets the stage for a positive atmosphere that radiates throughout the customer experience. When employees enjoy their work, their enthusiasm is contagious, creating a welcoming and upbeat environment that resonates with customers. Whether it's laughter, smiles, or playful banter, infusing a sense of fun into daily interactions fosters a warm and inviting atmosphere that customers are drawn to.

Building Rapport and Connection: Fun and laughter are universal languages that break down barriers and foster genuine connections. When employees engage in light-hearted interactions with customers, it humanises the service experience and creates a sense of camaraderie. Shared laughter and moments of levity build rapport, making customers feel more comfortable and valued as individuals.

Enhancing Creativity and Innovation: A playful work environment stimulates creativity and encourages innovative thinking. When employees feel free to express themselves and experiment with new ideas, they're more likely to come up with creative solutions to customer problems and anticipate their evolving needs. Fun sparks imagination and ingenuity, driving continuous improvement and innovation in the customer experience.

Boosting Morale and Motivation: Fun at work boosts employee morale and motivation, leading to higher levels of engagement and productivity. When employees enjoy coming to work and feel valued for their contributions, they're more invested in delivering exceptional service to customers. A positive work culture fosters a sense of pride and ownership, motivating employees to go above and beyond to create memorable experiences for customers.

Inspiring Loyalty and Advocacy: Customers remember experiences that evoke positive emotions and leave a lasting impression. When employees genuinely enjoy serving customers and inject a sense of fun into the interaction, it creates memorable moments that inspire loyalty and advocacy. Satisfied customers are more likely to return and recommend our business to others, driving growth and success in the long run.

Fostering Resilience and Adaptability: Fun at work fosters resilience and adaptability, enabling employees to navigate challenges with optimism and creativity. When faced with difficult situations or demanding customers, a playful mindset helps employees maintain perspective, stay focused, and find solutions with grace and composure.

Incorporating fun into the workplace is not just about having a good time - it's about creating an environment where employees thrive and customers reap the benefits. By adopting a culture of fun, engagement, and positivity, you can elevate the customer service experience from ordinary to exceptional, creating lasting memories and loyal advocates for your brand.

Creating a Positive First Impression

First impressions are formed within seconds of an encounter and can significantly influence the outcome of a customer interaction. Whether face-to-face or over the phone, creating a positive first impression sets the stage for a successful interaction and lays the foundation for a lasting relationship. Here are some practical strategies for making a memorable first impression in customer interactions:

Smile: It doesn't matter if you're on the phone or in person, smiling makes a difference. A customer can tell if you are interested or not by the way you sound and smiling can bring about a positive feel to the conversation. In person, a smile can help to show the customer that you are pleased to see them and pleased to be there.

Don't Sigh: When you answer the phone or you address a customer, don't start with a sigh. It will show that you aren't interested and even give the impression that the customer is interrupting your day. Sighing is one of the worst ways to start any interaction.

Warm and Professional Greeting: Begin the interaction with a warm and friendly greeting to make the customer feel welcome and valued. Whether face-to-face or on the phone, start with a smile in your voice and a genuine expression of interest in helping them. Use their name, if possible, to personalise the interaction and create a connection from the outset. For a phone interaction it could be: "Welcome to {COMPANY NAME}, you're speaking with {NAME}

Professional Appearance: If the interaction is face-to-face, pay attention to your appearance and conduct. Dress appropriately for the setting and maintain good posture and eye contact to convey confidence and professionalism. A neat and tidy appearance reflects positively on your professionalism and attention to detail.

Active Listening: Demonstrate active listening by giving the customer your full attention and refraining from distractions. Maintain eye contact, nod in acknowledgment, and use verbal cues such as "I understand" or "Please continue" to show that you're engaged and attentive to their needs. On the phone, listen for cues in their tone and demeanour to gauge their mood and adjust your approach accordingly.

Positive Language: Use positive and courteous language throughout the interaction to create a welcoming and professional atmosphere. Avoid negative or dismissive phrases and instead focus on offering solutions and assistance. For example, instead of saying "I can't help you with that," try "Let me find out what options are available for you."

Empathetic Response: If the customer expresses frustration or dissatisfaction, respond with empathy and understanding. Acknowledge their concerns and reassure them that you're committed to finding a solution. Empathetic responses help build trust and rapport, even in challenging situations.

Knowledge and Expertise: Demonstrate your knowledge and expertise by providing accurate information and helpful guidance. Be prepared to answer questions confidently and offer relevant solutions to meet the customer's needs. If you're unsure about something, don't hesitate to offer to find the information or assistance they require.

Follow-Up: At the end of the interaction, thank the customer for their time and assure them of your continued assistance if needed. Offer to follow up on any outstanding issues or inquiries to ensure their satisfaction. Following up demonstrates your commitment to customer care and reinforces the positive impression you've made.

It's important to show interest in the customer. Even if you're on the phone and someone comes into the reception area, you can silently acknowledge them before you wrap up your call. And if you're with someone in person and the phone rings, you shouldn't break off that conversation to take the call – it will give the impression that the phone call is more important than them.

Creating a positive first impression is essential for building trust, rapport, and satisfaction in customer interactions. By greeting customers warmly, demonstrating active listening, using positive language, and showcasing your knowledge and expertise, you can make a memorable impression that sets the stage for a successful relationship.

Positive Affirmations

When a customer reaches out to your organisation, whether by phone or in person, it presents an opportunity to instil confidence in your ability to provide assistance. One effective way to achieve this is by using positive affirmations - brief statements or greetings that reassure customers they are in capable hands and that their needs will be addressed promptly and effectively.

When greeting a customer, opt for a positive affirmation that conveys your readiness to assist. For instance, instead of a generic greeting, consider saying something like, "Welcome! I'm here to help you with any questions or concerns you may have today."

In addition, maintaining a positive disposition throughout the interaction is crucial. When a customer explains their situation, respond with enthusiasm and assurance. For instance, a simple yet effective phrase such as, "Absolutely, I can assist you with that," can go a long way in making the customer feel like they have come to the right place and feel valued.

In cases where another department or team may be better equipped to address the customer's needs, it's essential to frame the transfer positively. Rather than abruptly informing the customer that they've reached the wrong department, acknowledge their concern, and offer a helpful solution. For example, you might say, "I completely understand your situation. Our returns department specialises in handling these types of inquiries. Would you like me to connect you with them now?"

Importantly, avoid placing blame on the customer by insinuating that they've made a mistake in reaching out to the wrong department. Instead, adopt a customer-centric approach that acknowledges the customer's perspective. Remember, customers may not be familiar with the inner workings of your organisation, so it's crucial to guide them seamlessly to the appropriate resources without causing undue frustration or confusion.

By incorporating positive affirmations and maintaining a customer-focused mindset, you can create a welcoming and supportive environment that promotes trust and satisfaction among customers, ultimately enhancing their overall experience with your organisation.

Positive Responses

When you get into a conversation, there's an opportunity to maintain this positive approach by giving positive responses. As a customer service professional, you'll encounter customers seeking assistance for various reasons, and it's your expertise that shapes each interaction into a positive experience. Rather than starting off with a negative response, your goal is to reassure the customer by highlighting what you can do to address their needs.

Here are some ways to effectively turn potential negatives into positives:

Avoid Negative Language: Instead of leading with a "No," focus on the solutions and options available to the customer. For instance, instead of saying, "No, we can't help you as the technical team aren't in the office until next week," you could respond with, "Certainly, we're here to assist you. I'll ensure a technician reaches out to you promptly on Monday once they're back in the office."

Offer Solutions or Alternatives: Even if you can't fulfil the request immediately, provide reassurance by outlining a plan of action. For example, rather than bluntly stating, "No, we don't have that in stock," you can offer a solution such as, "While the item isn't currently in stock, we anticipate a delivery in two days. I'll arrange for it to be shipped to you on Friday."

Empathise and Provide Timely Updates: Acknowledge the customer's concern and keep them informed about the steps being taken to resolve their issue. This demonstrates attentiveness and builds trust. For instance, you could say, "I understand the urgency of your request. Rest assured, I'll keep you updated on the progress and ensure a swift resolution."

By reframing responses in a positive light and offering proactive solutions, you not only address the customer's immediate needs but also uphold a reputation for exceptional service.

Understanding and Managing Customer Needs

At the heart of every successful customer service interaction lies a deep understanding of the customer's needs and preferences. Managing customer needs effectively is not only essential for resolving issues and providing solutions but also for fostering trust, satisfaction, and loyalty. Heare are some ways to identify how understanding and managing customer needs can help you deliver excellent service.

Identifying Customer Needs: The first step in managing customer needs is to identify and understand them fully. Take the time to listen actively to the customer's concerns, ask probing questions to clarify their requirements, and empathise with their perspective. By gaining a comprehensive understanding of their needs, you can tailor your approach and solutions accordingly.

Prioritising Needs: Not all customer needs are equal - some may be urgent and require immediate attention, while others can be addressed over time. Prioritise customer needs based on their urgency, importance, and impact on the customer experience. By focusing on the most critical needs first, you can ensure that the customer's most pressing concerns are addressed promptly and effectively.

Customising Solutions: Once you've identified the customer's needs, tailor your solutions to meet their specific requirements and preferences. Offer personalised recommendations, alternative options, or customised services to address their unique situation. By providing tailored solutions, you demonstrate your commitment to meeting the customer's needs and exceeding their expectations.

Setting Realistic Expectations: Managing customer needs involves setting realistic expectations regarding what can be achieved and when. Be transparent about the timeline, resources, and limitations associated with the proposed solutions. Communicate clearly and honestly with the customer to ensure they have a realistic understanding of what to expect, thereby minimising disappointment or misunderstandings.

Anticipating Future Needs: As mentioned earlier, excellent service goes beyond addressing immediate needs - it involves anticipating and proactively addressing future needs as well. Anticipate potential challenges or issues that the customer may encounter down the line and offer pre-emptive solutions or recommendations to mitigate them. By staying one step ahead, you demonstrate foresight and commitment to the customer's long-term satisfaction.

Follow-Up and Feedback: After addressing the customer's needs, follow up to ensure their satisfaction and gather feedback on their experience. Use this feedback to continuously improve your service delivery and better meet the needs of future customers. Encourage customers to provide feedback and suggestions for improvement, demonstrating your commitment to ongoing excellence.

Building Relationships: Managing customer needs effectively is not just about solving problems - it's about building relationships based on trust, reliability, and mutual respect. By consistently meeting or exceeding their expectations, you foster loyalty and advocacy, turning satisfied customers into loyal brand ambassadors.

Managing customer needs effectively is fundamental to delivering excellent service and building lasting relationships. By understanding their needs, prioritising solutions, customising responses, setting realistic expectations, anticipating future needs, and seeking feedback, you can create positive experiences that resonate with customers and drive loyalty and advocacy.

Showing Empathy

Empathy is another building block of excellent customer service - it's the ability to understand and share the feelings of another person. In the realm of customer interactions, empathy plays a pivotal role in building trust, resolving issues, and creating positive experiences. Let's explore some practical strategies for showing empathy effectively in customer service interactions.

Active Listening: The foundation of empathy lies in active listening. Give your full attention to the customer, listen attentively to their concerns, and refrain from interrupting or rushing to provide solutions. Use verbal and nonverbal cues, such as nodding and paraphrasing, to demonstrate that you're fully engaged and understanding their perspective.

Validate Emotions: Acknowledge the customer's emotions and validate their feelings, even if you don't necessarily agree with their perspective. Express empathy by using phrases like "I understand how frustrating that must be" or "I can imagine that must have been upsetting." Validating emotions helps customers feel heard and respected, laying the groundwork for productive problem-solving.

Put Yourself in Their Shoes: Imagine yourself in the customer's situation and consider how you would feel if you were experiencing the same challenges. This exercise helps you empathise with their perspective and respond with greater sensitivity and understanding. Avoid making assumptions or judgments and instead focus on empathising with their unique circumstances.

Ask Open-Ended Questions: Encourage the customer to share more about their experience and feelings by asking open-ended questions. Instead of simply asking yes/no questions, invite them to elaborate on their concerns and preferences. This not only shows that you're interested in understanding their perspective but also allows them to express themselves more fully.

Use Empathetic Language: Choose your words carefully to convey empathy and understanding. Use phrases like "I'm here to help" or "I'm sorry you're experiencing this issue" to communicate your support and willingness to assist. Avoid using dismissive language or blaming the customer for the problem, as this can undermine their trust and exacerbate their frustration.

Empathise Without Overpromising: While it's essential to show empathy, be mindful not to overpromise or make commitments that you can't fulfil. Instead, focus on expressing empathy and reassuring the customer that you'll do your best to address their concerns. Be transparent about what you can realistically achieve and set clear expectations to avoid disappointment later.

Follow Up and Follow Through: After resolving the immediate issue, follow up with the customer to ensure their satisfaction and see if there's anything else you can assist them with. This demonstrates your continued commitment to their well-being and reinforces the positive impression you've made through your empathetic interactions. Follow through on any promises or commitments you've made to ensure a seamless resolution.

Empathy is a powerful tool for building connections, resolving conflicts, and creating memorable experiences in customer service interactions. By actively listening, validating emotions, and putting yourself in the customer's shoes, you can show empathy effectively and make a meaningful difference in their experience.

Communication Skills

Active Listening

Active listening is a foundational skill in customer service that goes beyond merely hearing what the customer is saying. It involves fully engaging with the customer, understanding their needs, and demonstrating empathy and concern. The topic of active listening comes up a number of times in this book as it is fundamental to providing an exceptional customer service. Here is a deeper look at what active listening actually entails.

Focused Attention: Active listening begins with giving the customer your undivided attention. Eliminate distractions, such as phones or other conversations, and focus solely on the customer and their needs. Maintain eye contact if you are in person, nod in acknowledgment, and use positive body language to convey attentiveness and receptiveness. If you're on the phone you can use minimal encouragers – these are verbal sounds like "Mmm" and "Ah huh" and "Yes". These things help people feel that you are listening, and they are an active engagement on your part.

Empathetic Understanding: Active listening requires more than just hearing words - it involves understanding the underlying emotions and concerns behind them. Put yourself in the customer's shoes and empathise with their perspective. Pay attention to their tone of voice, body language, and choice of words to gauge their emotional state and respond with empathy and compassion.

Clarifying and Paraphrasing: Clarify understanding by paraphrasing or summarising what the customer has said in your own words. This not only demonstrates that you're actively listening but also ensures that you've correctly interpreted their message. Use phrases like "If I understand correctly, you're saying..." or "Let me make sure I've got this right..." to confirm understanding and encourage further clarification if needed.

Asking Open-Ended Questions: Encourage the customer to elaborate on their concerns and preferences by asking open-ended questions. This allows them to express themselves more fully and provides valuable insights into their needs and expectations. Avoid leading questions or assumptions and instead let the customer guide the direction of the conversation.

Reflective Responses: Respond reflectively to the customer's concerns, acknowledging their feelings and validating their experiences. Use phrases like "I can understand why that would be frustrating" or "That sounds challenging" to express empathy and concern. Reflective responses reassure the customer that their feelings are heard and respected, laying the groundwork for constructive problem-solving.

Avoiding Interruptions: Resist the urge to interrupt or interject with your own thoughts or solutions while the customer is speaking. Allow them to express themselves fully without interruption, even if you already have a solution in mind. Interrupting can disrupt the flow of the conversation and make the customer feel unheard or dismissed.

Summarising and Confirming: At the conclusion of the conversation, summarise the key points discussed and confirm understanding with the customer. Recap the main issues, solutions proposed, and next steps agreed upon to ensure clarity and alignment. Confirm that the customer is satisfied with the resolution and address any remaining concerns before concluding the interaction.

Active listening is a fundamental skill in customer service that promotes understanding, empathy, and rapport. By giving the customer your full attention, empathising with their perspective, clarifying understanding, asking open-ended questions, providing reflective responses, avoiding interruptions, and summarising key points, you can create positive experiences that build trust and satisfaction.

Tone of Voice

Every interaction is a chance to make a lasting impression, therefore, the importance of tone cannot be overstated. Your tone of voice serves as a powerful tool that can either enhance or undermine the customer experience. Whether speaking in person, over the phone, or through written communication, the way you convey your message can significantly impact how it is received by the customer.

The adage "It's not what you say, but how you say it" holds significant merit when communicating with customers.

The way in which we convey a message, often referred to as the tone, can wield a greater influence than the actual words we use. It's the tone that permeates our words with meaning, conveying our emotions, intentions, and attitudes. Consider the simple question, "Who did this?" Depending on the tone employed, the same question can evoke vastly different responses from others.

Let's contrast two variations of the same inquiry: Somebody looking at a beautifully decorated thank you card saying "Who did this?" would be a very different tone to someone looking at a damaged parcel on a doorstep and shouting" Who did this?" The first carries a tone of mild curiosity or surprise, while the latter bristles with anger or frustration. It's evident that the tone we adopt can dramatically alter the way our message is perceived and received.

Even the inclusion of polite expressions like "please" isn't sufficient on its own. It's imperative that we align our tone with the intended message to effectively communicate with others. When engaging in dialogue, it's essential to be mindful of our tone, ensuring that it complements and reinforces the words we employ.

For instance, when offering a request, such as asking a colleague to complete a task, using a polite and respectful tone can foster cooperation and goodwill. Conversely, a harsh or impatient tone may elicit defensiveness or resistance, hindering productive communication.

In customer service interactions, the tone of voice assumes even greater significance. A warm and empathetic tone can reassure a frustrated customer and demonstrate genuine concern for their needs. Conversely, a dismissive or indifferent tone may exacerbate the customer's dissatisfaction, leading to further escalation of the issue.

In essence, your tone of voice serves as a powerful tool in interpersonal communication, shaping perceptions, influencing outcomes, and fostering meaningful connections. By paying attention to your tone and ensuring its alignment with your message, you can enhance the effectiveness of your communication and nurture positive relationships with others.

The tone of your voice plays a crucial role in establishing rapport with customers. A warm and friendly tone can instantly put the customer at ease and create a positive atmosphere for the interaction. For example, when greeting a customer, use a cheerful tone to convey sincerity and hospitality. Instead of a monotone "Hello," try saying, "Good morning! How can I assist you today?" This simple change in tone can make the customer feel valued and welcomed.

In situations where customers are expressing frustration or dissatisfaction, empathy is key. Your tone should convey understanding and concern for the customer's feelings. For instance, if a customer is experiencing difficulties with a product or service, respond with a compassionate tone that acknowledges their frustration. Rather than dismissing their concerns, say, "I'm truly sorry to hear about the inconvenience you've encountered. Let's work together to find a solution."

Customers often seek reassurance when faced with uncertainty or ambiguity. Your tone should convey confidence and competence to instil trust in your ability to assist them. For example, if a customer is unsure about a product's features, respond with a reassuring tone that exudes professionalism. Say, "Rest assured, our product comes with a comprehensive warranty to cover any issues you may encounter."

When dealing with irate or upset customers, maintaining a calm and composed tone is essential to de-escalate the situation. Avoid adopting a confrontational or defensive tone, as it can exacerbate tensions. Instead, respond with a calm and measured tone that seeks to find common ground. For example, if a customer is dissatisfied with a service outcome, acknowledge their concerns with a conciliatory tone. Say, "I understand your frustration, and I'm committed to resolving this issue to your satisfaction."

Finally, your tone should reflect gratitude and appreciation for the customer's business. A sincere and appreciative tone can leave a lasting impression and foster customer loyalty. When concluding the interaction, express your gratitude with a warm and thankful tone. Instead of a generic "Goodbye," say, "Thank you for choosing us! We appreciate your support and look forward to serving you again."

Your tone of voice is a powerful tool that can shape the customer experience in profound ways. By adopting the right tone, you can build rapport, convey empathy, provide assurance, resolve conflicts, and express appreciation effectively. Remember, every customer interaction is an opportunity to make a positive impact, so let your tone reflect your commitment to delivering exceptional service.

Intent and Impact

In every interaction, whether verbal or non-verbal, there exists a dual dynamic: the intended message and its resulting impact. However, it's common for these two facets to misalign, leading to misunderstandings and conflicts.

The intention behind communication represents the desired outcome or purpose behind conveying a message. Conversely, the impact of communication refers to the actual effect it has on the recipient. While we may have clarity about our own intentions, deciphering the intentions of others is often a murky endeavour. In turn, individuals cannot fully discern our intentions, relying solely on the observable impact of our words and actions.

The challenge arises when individuals combine the perceived impact with assumed intent. Upon experiencing a particular impact, whether positive or negative, there's a tendency to attribute it to the underlying intentions of the communicator. However, this assumption can lead to misinterpretations and strained relationships.

To mitigate the risk of misunderstanding, it's crucial to adopt a reflective approach. Rather than hastily attributing intentions to others, it's beneficial to engage in introspection and inquiry. By asking pertinent questions such as: What was explicitly said or done by the other person? How did it impact me emotionally or psychologically? What assumptions am I making about their intentions? - you can gain clarity and evaluate the validity of their assumptions.

Furthermore, it's imperative to recognise the shared nature of communication. Despite our best efforts to convey our intentions clearly, our words and actions may still yield unintended consequences. The impact of our communication on others can vary, influenced by factors such as tone, body language, and context. It's essential to remain cognizant of the potential for misinterpretation and strive to minimise adverse impacts.

Acknowledging the inherent complexity of human interaction, individuals must cultivate empathy and sensitivity towards others' experiences. Even in instances where intentions are noble, individuals may still experience hurt or discomfort due to the impact of communication. Validating these emotions and taking responsibility for our impact fosters understanding and facilitates constructive dialogue.

If a customer is yelling at you to get something sorted, their intention is likely to get a problem sorted. The impact may be to cause you to feel pain, sense of worthlessness or anger. Focusing on what the intention probably is will help you avoid reacting to what the impact was.

Slow Down your Speech when Needed

Speaking hastily can sometimes lead to confusion for your customers, ultimately undermining the effectiveness of your message.

To counteract this tendency and ensure clarity in communication, implementing strategies to moderate the pace of speech is essential. Here are several actionable steps to help slow down speech and enhance comprehension:

Adjust Your Speaking Speed: Recognise that the pace of conversation differs from that of formal presentations. Avoid the rapid tempo typical of informal dialogue and aim for a more measured approach, targeting an average rate of approximately 120 words per minute.

Practice Controlled Breathing: Nervousness or excitement can inadvertently accelerate speech. Counteract this tendency by cultivating controlled breathing techniques. Prior to talking to customers, take deliberate breaths to calm nerves and maintain a steady rhythm of speech.

Integrate intentional pauses into your delivery to allow listeners time to digest information. Utilise punctuation cues, such as commas and periods, to signal natural breaks in speech. These pauses not only facilitate comprehension but also lend emphasis to key points.

Provide Processing Time for customers: Recognise that effective communication involves more than just delivering information—it requires ensuring that recipients have sufficient time to process and internalise what is being conveyed. Allow brief intervals between sentences or ideas to enable listeners to absorb the content fully.

When sharing lists or sequences, deliberately pause for a moment after each item to allow listeners to mentally register the information. This deliberate pacing enhances retention and comprehension, particularly when conveying complex or detailed content.

All of these ideas can help with your own pacing but ultimately your customers will have an experience that is likely to be easier to understand and follow.

Controlling the Conversation

Every interaction is an opportunity to shape perceptions, build rapport, and ultimately, drive satisfaction. At the heart of these exchanges lies the delicate dance of conversation, where mastery lies in the ability to guide and control the flow of dialogue.

Imagine yourself as the conductor of an orchestra, orchestrating each note and tempo to create a harmonious melody. Similarly, in customer service, you are the maestro, leading the conversation with finesse and purpose.

Controlling the conversation is not about dominating or overpowering the customer; rather, it is about assuming the role of a trusted guide, steering them towards a resolution while ensuring their needs are met efficiently and effectively. Here's why it matters:

Efficiency: By taking the reins of the conversation, you can streamline the exchange, saving both time and resources. A well-controlled dialogue moves swiftly towards resolution, minimising unnecessary tangents and ensuring the customer's concerns are addressed promptly.

Clarity: When you control the conversation, you create a clear path for communication. By setting the agenda and guiding the discussion, you can avoid confusion and ambiguity, ensuring that both parties are on the same page and working towards a common goal.

Empowerment: Customers seek guidance and reassurance when they reach out for support. By assuming control of the conversation, you empower them with confidence in your expertise and ability to assist. Your proactive approach instils trust and cultivates a sense of security in the customer's mind.

Resolution: The goal of any customer service interaction is resolution. By controlling the conversation, you can steer it towards a satisfactory conclusion, addressing the customer's needs and concerns effectively. A well-managed dialogue ensures that no stone is left unturned in the quest for resolution.

So, how can you master the art of controlling conversations in customer service? Here are some key strategies to consider:

Set the Tone: Begin the conversation with a warm greeting and a confident attitude. Establish yourself as a knowledgeable and approachable resource, ready to assist the customer with their needs.

Active Listening: Listen attentively to the customer's concerns, paying close attention to their words, tone, and emotions. By demonstrating active listening skills, you signal to the customer that their voice is being heard and valued.

Ask Probing Questions: Guide the conversation by asking targeted questions that elicit relevant information. Use open-ended questions to encourage the customer to share their perspective and provide insights into their needs. If you need to get control of the conversation, ask a closed question as it will narrow the response bac from the customer.

Provide Guidance: Offer guidance and direction throughout the conversation, steering it towards a resolution. Share relevant information, offer recommendations, and outline next steps to move the dialogue forward.

Manage Expectations: Be transparent about what the customer can expect from the interaction, including timelines, processes, and potential outcomes. Managing expectations helps to avoid misunderstandings and ensures alignment between both parties.

Summarise and Confirm: Periodically summarise key points and confirm understanding to ensure clarity and alignment. Clarify any misconceptions or uncertainties and address any outstanding issues before concluding the conversation.

Remember, the key to effective conversation control lies in striking the right balance between assertiveness and empathy. By guiding the dialogue with confidence, empathy, and expertise, you can create positive and productive interactions that leave a lasting impression on the customer.

Keep your Customers Informed

Have you ever felt like your voice was lost in a sea of indifference when dealing with a business? Have you sent an email or made a call, only to hear nothing but silence in return? As customers, we crave acknowledgment and reassurance, yet all too often, our attempts at communication seem to vanish into thin air.

The importance of keeping customers informed cannot be overstated. It's not just about providing updates; it's about showing customers that their concerns matter and that their voices are heard. In today's competitive market, where customer loyalty is increasingly hard-won, businesses must prioritise clear and consistent communication to build trust and foster long-term relationships.

When a customer reaches out, whether through an email, a phone call, or a visit to your physical location, they are seeking resolution or assistance. By acknowledging their communication promptly and providing a timeframe for when they can expect a personalized response, you demonstrate respect for their time and concerns.

Research studies have shown that customers value timely responses and proactive communication. When customers feel ignored or left in the dark, it can lead to frustration and a loss of trust in your brand.

Consider this scenario: a customer sends an email or makes a call but receives no acknowledgment for several days. Naturally, they begin to doubt whether their message was received or if their concerns are being taken seriously. As the days pass without any response, their frustration grows, and they may even consider taking their business elsewhere.

Similarly, when customers are kept in the dark about delays or issues, it can lead to increased frustration and dissatisfaction. Whether it's a flight delay or a product shipment, customers appreciate honesty and transparency. Instead of stringing customers along with vague updates or false promises, businesses should strive to provide accurate and timely information, even if it's not what the customer wants to hear.

Research from First Financial Training Services has found that 96% of unhappy customers don't complain. However. 91% of those will simply leave and never come back. When customers feel like their concerns are not being addressed or their voices are not being heard, they are more likely to take their business elsewhere.

Remember, no news is still news. Even if there are no significant updates regarding a customer's issue, a simple acknowledgment can go a long way in reassuring them that their concerns have not been forgotten. By keeping customers informed every step of the way, businesses can mitigate frustration, build trust, and ultimately, retain valuable customers.

So, the next time a customer reaches out to you, remember that they are not just another number—they are the lifeblood of your business. Treat them with the respect and attention they deserve, and you'll reap the rewards of their loyalty and advocacy.

Fix the Customer First

One fundamental aspect often overlooked when dealing with customers is the immediate resolution of customer issues. Frequently, businesses unwittingly lose customers and jeopardise their reputation simply by failing to swiftly address customer concerns. This pivotal moment, often referred to as the "moment of truth," occurs when a customer encounters an unsatisfactory experience. The crucial approach here is to prioritise fixing the customer's immediate needs before delving into the root cause of the issue. Delaying resolution while attempting to pinpoint the cause can significantly aggravate the situation and lead to customer dissatisfaction. Shockingly, statistics reveal that a staggering 91% of dissatisfied customers are unlikely to engage with a business again.

Consider this scenario: At a local petrol station, a customer presents a discount coupon to offset the cost of their purchase. However, the attendant dismisses the coupon, citing an expiration date that had supposedly passed. Despite the customer's protestations and the mounting queue of impatient patrons, the attendant adamantly refuses to honour the coupon. Eventually, after much ado, the attendant begrudgingly accepts the coupon, leaving the customer exasperated and the other patrons disgruntled.

Regrettably, such scenarios are not uncommon and can be attributed to various factors, including inadequately trained staff, rigid company policies, and insufficient consideration for the customer's perspective. To illustrate further, let's explore a couple of hypothetical situations:

Imagine a small shop owner facing a malfunctioning drinks fridge supplied by a beverage producer. While the immediate problem lies with the faulty fridge, the underlying need is to ensure customers have access to chilled beverages. Instead of merely scheduling a repair, the producer could offer interim solutions, such as providing ice buckets, to address the immediate need for cold drinks.

Similarly, consider a printer company responding to a malfunctioning printer under contract. While dispatching a service technician is essential, the customer's primary concern remains the need for printed documents. Offering alternative printing solutions, such as loaner printers or outsourcing printing services, can mitigate the inconvenience caused by the printer downtime.

When confronted with dissatisfied customers, businesses must seize the opportunity to rectify the situation promptly. However, resolving customer issues goes beyond mere appeasement; it requires a systematic approach aimed at defusing tensions and restoring confidence. One effective strategy is the HEARD technique:

Hear: Allow the customer to express their grievances without interruption, demonstrating attentiveness and respect.

Empathise: Express empathy and understanding for the customer's frustration, validating their emotions.

Apologise: Offer a sincere apology for any inconvenience caused, irrespective of fault, to demonstrate accountability and goodwill.

Resolve: Take swift action to address the customer's concerns, seeking their input on potential solutions to ensure satisfaction.

Diagnose: Investigate the root cause of the issue to prevent recurrence, focusing on process improvements rather than assigning blame.

By adopting a customer-centric approach and prioritising immediate resolution, businesses can effectively mitigate customer dissatisfaction and foster long-term loyalty. In today's interconnected world, where customer perception profoundly influences brand reputation and success, prioritising customer needs is paramount.

To cultivate a customer-centric culture, businesses must align internal policies and practices with customer expectations. Instead of cumbersome procedures that inconvenience customers, companies should streamline processes and empower employees to make informed decisions. Try to give your employees decision making capability so they can sort our difficulties on the spot. Give them a financial threshold to offer discounts, refunds or discretionary payments so they can help build confidence in themselves and with the customers.

Furthermore, fostering a culture of empathy and respect towards both customers and employees can significantly enhance the overall customer experience.

The adage "fix the customer first" encapsulates a fundamental principle of customer service excellence. By promptly addressing customer concerns and prioritising their immediate needs, businesses can cultivate strong customer relationships and drive sustainable growth. Remember, in the customer service industry, customer satisfaction is the ultimate barometer of success.

Managing Difficult Customers

Difficult customer techniques

Interacting with difficult customers is an inevitable aspect of business, but with the right strategies, these encounters can be managed effectively to maintain positive relationships and uphold the reputation of the company. Here are some techniques for handling challenging customer interactions.

Understanding the Customer's Perspective: It's essential to recognise that every customer has their own reasons for complaining, and their expectations of service may vary. By acknowledging that we may not fully understand the customer's circumstances or emotions, we can approach interactions with empathy and open-mindedness. Remembering the Platinum Rule—"treat others the way they want to be treated"—underscores the importance of catering to individual preferences and needs.

Maintaining Composure and Empathy: When faced with an upset or angry customer, it's crucial to remain calm and composed, even in the face of demanding or confrontational behaviour. Rather than taking negative feedback personally, focus on listening attentively to the customer's concerns and validating their feelings. By demonstrating empathy and understanding, you can diffuse tension and establish a foundation for constructive dialogue.

The "Remind, Define, Diffuse" Process: A three-step process—remind, define, diffuse—can guide interactions with difficult customers. Begin by reminding yourself that the customer's frustration is directed at the situation, not you personally. Avoid becoming defensive and instead focus on active listening and note-taking to understand the root cause of their dissatisfaction. Next, define the issue clearly by clarifying the customer's concerns and confirming your understanding. Finally, diffuse the situation by expressing empathy and offering solutions or reassurances to address their needs.

The "Sorry, Glad, Sure" Technique: To further defuse emotional tension and reassure the customer, employ the "sorry, glad, sure" technique. Start by expressing genuine apologies for any inconvenience or frustration the customer has experienced. Acknowledge their concerns and show appreciation for bringing the issue to your attention, demonstrating a commitment to resolution. Finally, express confidence in your ability to address the problem and offer assistance, reinforcing the customer's confidence in your willingness to help. The three-step process can sound like this. "I'm sorry to hear that's happened. I'm glad you brought it to our attention. I'm sure there's something we can do about it."

The L.A.S.T. Approach: Another effective framework for managing difficult customers is the L.A.S.T. approach - Listen, Acknowledge, Solve, Thank. Begin by actively listening to the customer's grievances without interruption, allowing them to express their concerns fully. Acknowledge their feelings and validate their experiences, showing empathy and understanding. Next, work towards resolving the issue by following established procedures or seeking assistance as needed. Finally, express gratitude to the customer for bringing the matter to your attention and demonstrating their commitment to resolution.

Closing the Conversation: Once the issue has been addressed satisfactorily, it's important to close the conversation on a positive note. Gain agreement from the customer regarding the proposed solution or actions, ensuring clarity and understanding.

Paraphrase the key points of the conversation to confirm alignment and demonstrate active listening. Use the customer's name to personalise the interaction and show appreciation for their cooperation. Finally, express commitment to ongoing support and help with any additional needs, concluding the interaction with gratitude and professionalism.

By applying these techniques and approaches, businesses can effectively manage difficult customer interactions, mitigate tensions, and uphold the integrity of the customer relationship.

Handling Abusive Customers

Encountering abusive customers can be challenging and distressing, but with the right techniques and approaches, these situations can be managed effectively while preserving professionalism and ensuring the well-being of employees. Abusive customers are those who might be shouting, using an aggressive tone or foul language, calling you unpleasant names, or are threatening you. Let's look at navigating interactions with abusive customers, including understanding the root causes of abusive behaviour, preventing escalation, and responding assertively while prioritising safety and well-being.

Understanding the Source of Abusive Behaviour: Abusive behaviour often stems from underlying emotions such as anger, frustration, or feelings of helplessness. Customers may resort to abusive behaviour as a means of exerting control, venting their emotions, or seeking restitution for perceived grievances. It's important to recognise that while these emotions are valid, abusive behaviour is not acceptable and should be addressed promptly and assertively.

Preventing Escalation: The key to managing interactions with abusive customers is to take charge of the conversation from the outset and prevent escalation. Begin by maintaining confidence and professionalism, regardless of the customer's behaviour. Avoid becoming defensive or retaliatory, as this can escalate tensions and exacerbate the situation. Instead, focus on de-escalation techniques and assertive communication to assert boundaries and maintain control of the interaction.

Identifying Verbal and Nonverbal Abuse: Verbal abuse encompasses a range of behaviours, from explicit swearing and yelling to personal attacks and accusations. Nonverbal abuse may manifest through intimidating body language, aggressive gestures, or menacing facial expressions. Recognising these signs of abuse is essential for addressing the behaviour effectively and implementing appropriate response strategies.

Responding Assertively and Safely: When faced with abusive behaviour, it's crucial to respond assertively while prioritising safety and well-being. Begin by acknowledging the customer's emotions and concerns without condoning their abusive behaviour. Set clear boundaries and assertively communicate expectations for respectful behaviour. If the abusive behaviour persists, escalate the situation by alerting supervisor or security personnel and removing yourself from the interaction if necessary.

Terminating the Interaction: In cases of persistent or escalating abuse, it may be necessary to terminate the interaction to ensure the safety and well-being of employees. Begin by alerting the customer to the impact of their behaviour and providing clear warnings about the consequences of continued abuse. If the behaviour persists despite interventions, take decisive action to terminate the interaction and seek assistance from appropriate authorities or support personnel. You do not have to put up with such behaviour. Always follow your company procedures and consider these steps:

Firstly, remain calm, polite, and in control. Remind them you are trying to help. Tell them their behaviour is not acceptable and that it isn't helping. If they persist, remind them you have advised them about the behaviour and will terminate the conversation if they continue. If they persist further, explain that you have already advised them twice that their behaviour is unacceptable and will now terminate the conversation. Log the incident and inform your manager.

Documentation and Reporting: Following interactions with abusive customers, it's essential to document the incident and report it to relevant stakeholders, such as supervisors or managers. Record details of the interaction, including the customer's behaviour, any threats or intimidation, and the actions taken to address the situation. This documentation serves as a valuable record for future reference and can inform policies and procedures for handling similar situations in the future.

Employee Support and Well-being: Finally, prioritise the well-being of employees who may experience distress or trauma as a result of abusive interactions. Offer support and resources for coping with stress and managing emotional reactions. Provide training and guidance on self-care techniques and encourage open communication about challenging interactions to foster a supportive and resilient workplace culture.

Dealing with Emotional Customers

Dealing with emotional customers can present significant challenges, often leaving individuals feeling unprepared and uncertain about how to navigate such interactions. The unpredictability of emotions and the potential intensity of these encounters can make them daunting for many. However, with careful preparation and a compassionate approach, you can effectively manage these situations and foster positive outcomes for both you and the client.

Emotional distress, stemming from traumatic events or life-altering circumstances, can manifest in various forms, including grief, anxiety, anger, or depression. These experiences significantly impact individuals' emotional well-being and may influence their behaviour and communication style. As a result, emotional clients may exhibit a range of reactions, from tearful outbursts to expressions of frustration or aggression.

Understanding the underlying factors driving these emotional responses is crucial for effectively managing customer interactions. Whether the customer is grappling with the loss of a loved one, navigating a difficult life transition, or coping with personal challenges, empathy and sensitivity are paramount. By acknowledging the customer's emotional state and validating their feelings, you can establish trust and rapport, laying the foundation for constructive dialogue and problem-solving.

When engaging with emotional customers, it's essential to adopt a proactive and empathetic approach. Here are some strategies to consider:

Maintain Emotional Regulation: Prioritise self-awareness and emotional regulation to effectively support customers in distress. Practice deep breathing techniques to manage stress and maintain composure during challenging interactions. Remember that your attitude and tone can profoundly impact the customer's emotional state, so strive to convey calmness and empathy.

Demonstrate Empathy: Validate the customer's emotions and demonstrate empathy by actively listening to their concerns without judgment. Use empathetic phrases such as "I understand this must be difficult for you" or "I'm here to support you through this." By acknowledging the client's emotional experience, you create a safe space for them to express their feelings openly.

Practice Active Listening: Engage in active listening to demonstrate genuine interest and understanding. Allow the customer to express themselves fully and validate their experiences. Avoid interrupting or imposing your own judgments, and instead, focus on creating a supportive environment where the client feels heard and valued.

Offer Practical Support: Provide practical assistance and reassurance to alleviate the customer's immediate concerns. Offer concrete solutions or resources to address their needs and facilitate problem-solving. Whether it's assisting with paperwork, offering information, or connecting them with relevant support services, demonstrate your commitment to supporting their well-being.

Respect Boundaries: Recognise the customer's boundaries and comfort levels and avoid pressuring them to disclose more than they're comfortable sharing. Respect their privacy and autonomy and prioritise their emotional well-being throughout the interaction. Avoid making assumptions or offering unsolicited advice, and instead, focus on creating a supportive and non-judgmental space for them to express themselves.

Follow-Up and Check-In: After the initial interaction and if appropriate, follow up with the customer to express continued support and inquire about their well-being. Demonstrate genuine care and concern by checking in periodically and offering assistance as needed. By maintaining ongoing communication and support, you can reinforce trust and strengthen the client-provider relationship.

Vulnerable customers

Vulnerable customers encompass a broad spectrum of individuals who may face challenges or limitations that affect their ability to engage effectively in commercial transactions. These challenges could stem from various factors such as age, physical or mental infirmity, minority status, temporary conditions, or other forms of disempowerment.

In serving vulnerable customers, it's important to adopt a compassionate and inclusive approach. Here's how you can assist them effectively:

Active Listening: Take the time to truly listen to vulnerable customers. Pay attention to their verbal and non-verbal cues to gauge their level of comprehension and engagement. Avoid rushing through interactions and allow them the opportunity to express themselves fully.

Avoid Assumptions: Refrain from making assumptions about the capabilities or preferences of vulnerable customers. Instead, approach each interaction with an open mind and a willingness to adapt your communication style to meet their needs.

Encourage Participation: Create a supportive environment where vulnerable customers feel empowered to participate in the discussion. Offer them opportunities to ask questions, seek clarification, and share their concerns. Validate their contributions and ensure they feel heard and valued.

Respect Communication Preferences: Respect the communication preferences of vulnerable customers and accommodate them to the best of your ability. Whether they prefer verbal communication, written correspondence, or alternative formats, strive to meet their needs and preferences.

Collaborative Problem-Solving: Invite vulnerable customers to collaborate with you in finding solutions to their challenges. Use phrases like "Can I suggest..." or "May I offer to..." to propose helpful suggestions or assistance. Empower them to actively engage in decision-making processes that affect them.

Summarise and Clarify: At the conclusion of each interaction, summarise the key points discussed and clarify any actions or next steps required. Ensure that vulnerable customers have a clear understanding of the information exchanged and feel confident about the agreed-upon course of action.

Coping Under Fire

Serving in frontline roles such as those in call centres, reception desks, retail, or other customer service positions can often feel like navigating through a relentless storm of demands, with little acknowledgment for the efforts invested. Amidst these pressures, mastering the art of 'coping under fire' becomes essential. Here are some invaluable strategies to navigate the tumultuous waters of customer service:

Firstly, it's crucial to remember that the frustrations and challenges encountered by customers are not directed at you personally. Taking a step back and recognising that you are not the cause of their issues can provide a valuable perspective. Instead of rushing in defensively, take a deep breath and allow customers the space to express their concerns. Many simply need an outlet to vent their frustrations, and by offering a listening ear, you can demonstrate empathy and understanding.

Empathy is the cornerstone of effective customer service. People crave acknowledgment and validation, especially when facing difficulties. By genuinely empathising with customers' experiences, you can create a connection that transcends the transactional nature of the interaction. Listen attentively to their concerns and reflect back on what they've shared to show that you genuinely care about finding a resolution.

Maintaining self-awareness is paramount in high-pressure situations. Pay close attention to your tone of voice, body language, and reactions. Avoid sighing, speaking in an escalated tone, or displaying signs of frustration, as these behaviours can exacerbate tensions and escalate conflicts. Instead, strive to remain composed, patient, and composed, even in the face of adversity.

Lastly, prioritise your well-being by incorporating regular breaks into your day. Even brief moments of respite can provide much-needed relief from the intensity of customer interactions. Use these breaks to engage in a reward task or activity that brings you joy or relaxation. Whether it's taking a short walk, enjoying a warm or cool drink, or practicing mindfulness exercises, investing in self-care is essential for sustaining resilience and managing stress effectively.

Handling Customer Escalations Effectively

In any customer-facing role, whether as a manager or a team member, dealing with escalations is an inevitable part of the job. Customers may request to speak with a supervisor, often perceiving it as a quicker way to resolve their issues or concerns. However, there are proactive steps you can take to address customer concerns effectively and potentially avoid unnecessary escalations.

Demonstrate Empathy and Acknowledgment: Begin by acknowledging the customer's situation and expressing empathy for their frustration or concern. This simple act can go a long way in defusing tensions and building trust.

Establish Your Authority and Capability: Reassure the customer that you have the authority and capability to handle their request or inquiry. This can be done through a phrase like, "I have the necessary expertise and authority to assist you with your request. Please allow me the opportunity to address your concerns."

Offer a Conditional Escalation: If the customer remains unsatisfied after your initial efforts, you can offer a conditional escalation. This approach demonstrates your willingness to involve a supervisor, if necessary, while still giving you the opportunity to resolve the issue yourself. A phrase like, "I'll be glad to assist you with your request. If you feel that further assistance is needed after our interaction, I can then transfer you to my supervisor."

Avoid Dismissive Language: Be mindful of using phrases that may come across as dismissive or minimizing the customer's concerns. Statements like "My supervisor is only going to say the same thing" can be counterproductive and may escalate the situation further.

By following these steps, you can effectively manage customer escalations, build trust, and demonstrate your commitment to resolving their concerns. Remember, a proactive and empathetic approach can often defuse tensions and lead to a more positive outcome for both the customer and your organization.

Specific Customer Service Tips

As well as overall ideas on how to help attract customers and keep them through an excellent service experience, some simple tactical tips for specific needs can be useful. This next section deals with some great specific tips to help you handle situations like giving bade news, saying no in a good way and dealing with various types of difficult customers.

Delivering Bad News

In customer service, there are occasions when the information you provide may not align with the customer's expectations or preferences, resulting in what could be perceived as "bad news." However, how this news is delivered can significantly influence the customer's perception and overall experience. Here are some strategies for delivering bad news in a way that maintains positivity and fosters constructive outcomes for both the customer and the business.

When delivering news that may be unfavourable to the customer, it's essential to acknowledge the potential impact on their expectations and emotions. Whether it's informing them of an unexpected charge or a delay in service, being mindful of their perspective can help guide the communication process and mitigate negative reactions.

The concept of delivering bad news followed by good news can be a valuable tool in managing customer expectations and perceptions. By coupling the unfavourable information with a positive alternative or solution, you can soften the blow and offer a sense of hope or reassurance to the customer. For example, if informing a customer of an overdue payment, you can follow up with the option of setting up a flexible payment plan to accommodate their financial situation. As an example, you may have to tell a customer they owe some money. That's the bad news. The good news is that they may have some time to pay it back. It may sound like this:

"You do actually owe $300 on your account. However, if you can't pay that in full now, I am happy to set up a payment plan to help you."

Or,

"You've missed the cut-off for a delivery tomorrow. However, we do open early on the weekends if you'd like to collect."

The language and tone used when delivering bad news play a crucial role in shaping the customer's response and overall experience. Instead of framing the information in a negative light, focus on conveying empathy, understanding, and a willingness to assist. Use phrases that convey sincerity and a commitment to finding a resolution, such as "I understand this may not be what you were expecting, but I'm here to help find a solution that works for you."

Providing examples of positive messaging can help customer service representatives navigate challenging conversations with confidence and professionalism. For instance, when informing a customer of a missed delivery deadline, you can offer alternatives such as early weekend pickup options to accommodate their needs. By highlighting alternative solutions or options, you can empower the customer to act and move forward positively.

Developing sample scripts for delivering bad news can provide customer service representatives with a framework for effectively communicating sensitive information. These scripts should incorporate elements of empathy, positivity, and problem-solving, ensuring that the customer feels supported and valued throughout the interaction. For instance, when informing a customer of a billing discrepancy, the script could include acknowledgment of the issue followed by reassurance of assistance in resolving it.

To enhance proficiency in delivering bad news with a positive spin, businesses can implement training programs and role-playing exercises for customer service teams. These activities allow employees to practice communication strategies in simulated scenarios and receive feedback on their approach. By honing their skills in empathy, active listening, and effective messaging, employees can confidently navigate challenging conversations with customers and uphold the organisation's reputation for exceptional service.

By adopting a proactive approach to delivering bad news and emphasising positivity in communication, businesses can transform potentially negative interactions into opportunities to strengthen customer relationships and loyalty.

How to Say No Nicely

When faced with a situation where you must decline a customer's request, it's essential to remember that saying no doesn't have to entail being rude or unhelpful. Instead, you can maintain a positive attitude and ensure the customer feels respected and valued throughout the interaction. By following a simple four-step process, you can gracefully decline the request while offering alternatives where possible.

The first step is to acknowledge the customer's request sincerely. This demonstrates empathy and understanding of their needs, even if you are unable to fulfil them entirely. Once you've acknowledged their request, you can politely decline while providing clear and honest reasons for doing so. Transparency is key in building trust and credibility with the customer.

For instance, imagine a scenario where a customer requests a delivery by 10 AM the next day. While you may not be able to guarantee such a prompt delivery due to logistical constraints, you can explain this to the customer in a respectful manner.

After declining the request, the next step is to offer alternatives whenever possible. This shows the customer that you are committed to finding a solution that meets their needs, even if it may not align with their initial request. Continuing with the example, you could propose alternative delivery options such as a 12:00

noon delivery directly to the site address or the option to pay for an express service for a dedicated courier delivery before 10 AM.

You might say something like this:

"I understand how urgently you need that item. However, in this instance, I cannot guarantee a 10 AM delivery as the item will be coming from another depot outside of our normal courier service area. What I can do is offer you a 12:00 noon delivery straight to the site address. Or if you would like to pay for an express service, we can organise a dedicated courier to you before 10 AM."

By following these four easy steps - acknowledge, decline, provide reasons, and offer alternatives - you can effectively navigate situations where you must say no to a customer's request. With practice, this approach becomes second nature, allowing you to maintain professionalism and positivity in all customer interactions. Remember, the goal is to ensure the customer feels heard, respected, and supported, even when their request cannot be accommodated precisely as they desire.

Dealing with Knowledgeable customers

Customers who demonstrate a high level of knowledge or expertise in your industry or organisation can present unique challenges and opportunities for customer service professionals. By recognising and leveraging their expertise, you can enhance the quality of your interactions and build stronger relationships. Here are five strategies to effectively engage with knowledgeable customers:

Acknowledge Their Expertise: Start by acknowledging the customer's knowledge and experience in the industry or organisation. Phrases such as "As you would appreciate" or "As you would be aware" demonstrate respect for their level of expertise and establish a foundation for productive dialogue.

Ask Open and Probing Questions: Engage the customer in meaningful conversation by asking open-ended and probing questions. Encourage them to share their insights and perspectives by starting sentences with phrases like "Tell me more about this." This approach fosters a collaborative exchange of information and demonstrates your interest in their expertise.

Be Firm yet Polite: Maintain a balance of assertiveness and politeness when interacting with knowledgeable customers. Clearly communicate your needs and requirements by using phrases like "In order to assist you effectively, I need to understand the following." Firmness ensures clarity and efficiency in communication, while politeness reinforces professionalism and respect.

Practice Honesty: Ensure transparency and integrity in your interactions by refraining from lying or providing inaccurate information. If you're unsure about a particular issue, don't hesitate to consult with a colleague or supervisor for clarification. Honesty builds trust and credibility, fostering a positive customer experience.

Know Your Boundaries and Authority: Understand the scope of your responsibilities and the limits of your authority to act. Clarify any boundaries or constraints that may impact your ability to address the customer's needs effectively. Knowing your boundaries allows you to manage expectations appropriately and prevent misunderstandings.

By implementing these strategies, you can navigate interactions with knowledgeable customers with confidence and professionalism, encouraging mutual respect and collaboration.

Effectively Managing Talkative Customers

Encountering talkative customers who tend to stray from the initial query can pose challenges, especially when time is limited, or other customers are waiting. However, with the right strategies, you can guide the conversation back on track while ensuring the customer feels heard and valued. Here are some key tips to effectively manage talkative customers:

Establish Control of the Conversation: Take control of the conversation from the outset by asking closed questions that prompt specific responses. For instance, you might begin by asking, "Is this problem occurring right now?" This approach helps steer the conversation in a focused direction and prevents the customer from veering off topic.

Utilise Paraphrasing Techniques: Use paraphrasing techniques to summarise the customer's issue and prompt a concise response. By paraphrasing the problem back to the customer, you encourage them to provide a one-word answer, facilitating clearer communication and efficient resolution. For example, you could say, "So if I understand correctly, you're experiencing..."

Practice Active Listening: Engage in active listening throughout the conversation to demonstrate empathy and attentiveness. Pay close attention to the customer's concerns, questions, and feedback, and respond thoughtfully to demonstrate your commitment to addressing their needs. By listening attentively, you validate the customer's perspective and foster a sense of trust and understanding.

Adjust Your Speaking Pace: Adapt your speaking pace to match the customer's communication style and effectively manage the flow of the conversation. Speaking slowly can help slow down the customer's pace, making it easier to guide the discussion back to the main issue at hand. By maintaining a calm and deliberate speaking pace, you create a sense of control and professionalism in the interaction.

Conclude the Conversation Appropriately: Once the customer's issue has been addressed satisfactorily, conclude the conversation in a courteous and professional manner. Express gratitude for the opportunity to assist the customer and reassure them that their needs have been met. For instance, you might say, "Thank you for reaching out. I'm glad we could resolve your issue today."

These strategies can help you navigate interactions with talkative customers confidently and efficiently, ensuring a positive experience for both the customer and you. Remember to remain patient, attentive, and proactive in guiding the conversation toward resolution.

Minimising Customer Effort

Customer effort refers to the level of difficulty or exertion required by customers to resolve issues, fulfil requests, or obtain information from a company. It is measured through the customer effort score, calculated as a percentage, where lower scores indicate less effort, and higher scores indicate greater effort. In today's competitive landscape, minimising customer effort is crucial for retaining customers and fostering loyalty. Customers prefer seamless and effortless transactions, and they are more likely to switch to competitors if they encounter obstacles or frustrations in their interactions.

To improve customer effort scores and enhance the overall customer experience, businesses can implement the following strategies:

Offer Multiple Contact Channels: Provide customers with various channels for communication and feedback, such as phone, email, live chat, and social media. Let customers choose the channel that best suits their preferences and needs, ensuring accessibility and convenience.

Utilise Self-Service Tools: Empower customers to find solutions independently by offering self-service options, such as FAQs, knowledge bases, tutorials, and troubleshooting guides. Make these resources easily accessible and user-friendly, allowing customers to resolve issues quickly and efficiently on their own.

Reduce Wait Times: Minimise wait times for customer inquiries and support requests by optimising staffing levels, implementing efficient queuing systems, and streamlining internal processes. Promptly respond to customer queries and strive to resolve issues in a timely manner, minimising frustration and enhancing satisfaction.

Simplify Contact Processes: Make it easy for customers to reach the appropriate department or representative by simplifying contact processes. Provide clear instructions for contacting support, routing inquiries effectively, and minimising unnecessary steps or transfers.

Be Proactive: Take a proactive approach to customer service by anticipating customer needs and addressing potential issues before they arise. Proactively reach out to customers with relevant information, updates, or offers, demonstrating attentiveness and commitment to their satisfaction.

Lead the Conversation: Assume a leadership role in customer interactions by guiding the conversation and taking proactive steps to assist customers. Listen actively to their concerns, offer personalised recommendations or solutions, and facilitate a seamless and positive experience from start to finish.

By implementing these strategies, you can minimise customer effort, enhance the customer experience, and foster long-term loyalty and satisfaction. Prioritising ease of interaction and proactively addressing customer needs are essential components of building strong and mutually beneficial relationships with customers.

Think of how you want to be treated as a customer. You expect to be guided to the best outcome without having to do all the work or all the thinking. You expect the business you're dealing with o be the experts. In your role, try to help the customer feel like you are doing the work. You can make the suggestions and help them towards the best end result.

First contact Resolution

Experiencing the frustration of contacting an organisation multiple times to resolve an issue or query is a common gripe among customers. It not only undermines their confidence in the organisation but also risks tarnishing the brand's reputation and potentially driving customers away. Reflect on your own experiences as a customer. Have you ever had to reach out to an organisation with a problem or question? How seamless was the process, and were you able to get your issue resolved on the first attempt?

For many customers, encountering difficulties in resolving their concerns during initial contact can be disheartening. It not only disrupts their experience but also prompts them to reach out to the organisation repeatedly to find a resolution. Unfortunately, this often results in frustration and dissatisfaction, leading customers to question their future dealings with the organisation.

Consider the implications of failing to address customer queries effectively during the first contact. Firstly, it detracts from the overall customer experience, leaving a negative impression that can impact brand loyalty. Secondly, it increases the likelihood of customers initiating further contact to seek resolution, perpetuating the cycle of frustration. Additionally, if customers are prompted to complete a satisfaction survey, a lack of first-contact resolution may lead to lower ratings, further affecting the organisation's reputation.

First Contact Resolution (FCR) is a crucial metric, particularly in contact centres, where the goal is to resolve customer issues promptly and efficiently. However, the principles of FCR can be applied across all departments within an organisation to enhance customer satisfaction. The key is to prioritise resolving customer queries effectively during the initial interaction to minimise the need for follow-up contacts.

Research indicates that 12% of customers may defect if their issues require two or more calls to resolve. Therefore, it's essential to assess your organisation's FCR performance and identify areas for improvement. By measuring FCR, organisations can gauge their effectiveness in resolving customer issues on the first attempt, thereby saving both time and resources.

Measuring FCR involves tracking the number of customer contacts that result in a resolution during the initial interaction. While internal metrics provide valuable insights for process improvement, gathering true customer feedback through surveys is essential for assessing satisfaction levels. It's crucial to solicit feedback from customers to ensure that their concerns are adequately addressed and resolved to their satisfaction.

To improve FCR, organisations should empower their staff to make decisions and resolve issues quickly. Training programs should equip employees with the skills and knowledge needed to handle common queries effectively. Coaching sessions can address scenarios that may lead to multiple contacts about the same issue, while discussion forums facilitate the sharing of ideas for quick resolution.

Regardless of your role within the organisation, it's helpful to go the extra mile for customers. Anticipate their needs and provide value-added assistance, such as directing them to self-service options or providing relevant information proactively. By prioritising first-contact resolution and striving to exceed customer expectations, organisations can enhance their reputation, raise customer loyalty, and drive business growth.

Going the Extra Mile: Adding Value to Customer Inquiries

When responding to a customer inquiry, you have a valuable opportunity to enhance the customer experience by providing additional information or benefits that go beyond simply addressing their initial request. By taking the time to consider what else might be helpful or valuable to the customer, you can demonstrate your commitment to exceptional service and build lasting relationships.

Anticipate Future Needs: Look beyond the immediate inquiry and consider what other information or resources might assist the customer in the future. For example, you could provide self-service information available on your website or share shortcuts to streamline processes, saving them time and effort down the line.

Highlight Relevant Offers and Alternatives: Keep an eye out for special offers, promotions, or alternative options that the customer may not be aware of but could benefit from. Whether it's a discount, a complementary service, or a more suitable product or service, presenting these options can add significant value to the customer's experience.

Facilitate Seamless Follow-Up: If the customer needs to follow up or reach out again, make the process as smooth as possible. Provide them with a reference number, a direct contact, or a dedicated phone line to expedite future interactions, minimizing frustration and demonstrating your commitment to efficient service.

Personalize the Experience: While adding value is essential, it's crucial to ensure that the additional information or benefits you provide are relevant and tailored to the specific customer's needs and preferences. Avoid generic, one-size-fits-all responses that may come across as impersonal or irrelevant.

Seek Continuous Improvement: Regularly review your customer interactions and seek feedback to identify opportunities for improvement. Stay up to date with industry trends, best practices, and customer preferences to ensure that the value you offer remains relevant and impactful.

By consistently going the extra mile and adding value to customer inquiries, you not only enhance the overall customer experience but also further loyalty, trust, and long-lasting relationships. This approach sets you apart from competitors and demonstrates your commitment to exceptional service, ultimately contributing to the success and growth of your organization.

Moments of Truth

Moments of Truth are pivotal junctures in a customer's interaction with a brand or product, wielding significant influence over their perception and future decisions. You can find some great ideas of this concept in the book, "Moments of Truth" by Jan Carlzon. Here are some key components of this concept:

Moments of Glory: These moments shine brightest when service surpasses expectations, leaving a lasting positive impression on the customer. Examples:

• During the initial encounter, receiving a discount coupon for purchasing a SAAS software service from a website.

• Post-purchase, reaching out to offer guidance and support with setup or usage.

• In brick-and-mortar establishments like restaurants, offering complimentary beverages to patrons awaiting their orders.

Moments of Pain: Conversely, moments of pain denote unfortunate interactions that heighten the risk of customer dissatisfaction and attrition. Examples:

- Encountering a rude customer service representative during a phone call.

- Being overlooked by a retail salesperson despite seeking assistance in-store.

However, adept handling of moments of pain can transform them into remarkable customer experiences by swiftly addressing and resolving issues. Going the extra mile to assist customers not only rectifies the situation but also deepens their loyalty to the brand. Imagine being in a cafe where the waiter apologises for delays and presents a "Sorry card" with a discount for the subsequent order. Why do Moments of Truth matter?

Positive Moments of Truth: Skilful navigation advances enduring brand loyalty and advocacy.

Negative Moments of Truth: Mishandling these instances jeopardises customer retention and potentially damages your brand's reputation.

Bear in mind that these moments wield immense influence over a customer's decision to continue their engagement with your brand. Therefore, strive for excellence in every critical interaction!

Every interaction we have with a customer presents a crucial moment of truth, providing us with an opportunity to not just meet but exceed their expectations while adding significant value to their experience. Here are some steps to ensure we make the most of these moments:

Personalise the Contact: Addressing the customer by name and demonstrating genuine interest in their needs sets a positive tone for the interaction. For instance, "Thank you for reaching out, Mr. Smith. How may I assist you today?"

Make a Positive First Impression: The initial moments of the conversation are pivotal. Expressing warmth and professionalism can leave a lasting impression. For example, "I'm here to help you with your query, Mr. Smith, and I'm committed to ensuring your satisfaction."

Look for Opportunities to Add Value: Beyond addressing the customer's immediate request, seek ways to enhance their experience. For instance, "I've noticed that you don't currently have the ACME 1 product. Considering its benefits, I've taken the liberty of emailing you the details for your review. This could provide valuable insights for your future needs."

Anticipate Unspoken Needs: Proactively identifying potential concerns or additional assistance the customer may require demonstrates attentiveness and care. For example, "Before we conclude, is there anything else I can assist you with today? Your satisfaction is our priority."

Each interaction becomes an opportunity to not just meet expectations but to exceed them, leaving customers happy and satisfied every time.

Product and Service Knowledge

A robust understanding of products and services forms the bedrock of exceptional sales and service experiences. It instils confidence in handling customer inquiries and ensures satisfaction in delivering optimal solutions.

Staying abreast of updates and enhancements can be challenging and this underscores the importance of developing comprehensive product manuals, both in physical and digital formats. Moreover, leveraging the knowledge and expertise of colleagues can serve as a valuable resource in filling gaps and gaining insights.

Confidence is a key trait of effective customer interactions. Uncertainty or ambiguity can undermine credibility and erode trust. Rather than resorting to vague responses or guesswork, it is essential to exude confidence in discussing your products and services. If faced with uncertainty, gracefully acknowledge the need to verify information and assure the customer of your commitment to providing accurate answers. Adopting phrases like "Let me verify that for you" demonstrates professionalism and instils confidence in the customer.

Product and service knowledge encompasses a deep understanding of the offerings provided by an organisation, spanning both tangible products and intangible services. It involves familiarity with the features, functionalities, benefits, and specifications of each offering, allowing service providers to effectively communicate their value to customers. Product knowledge entails being well-versed in the physical attributes and capabilities of products, including their design, composition, and technical specifications. On the other hand, service knowledge pertains to an understanding of the range of services offered by a company, such as customer support, maintenance, or consultancy, as well as the processes and procedures associated with delivering these services. Together, product and service knowledge equip service providers with the expertise needed to address customer inquiries, offer tailored recommendations, and provide solutions that meet the unique needs and preferences of each customer.

In addition, product and service knowledge extends beyond mere familiarity with the offerings themselves; it also encompasses awareness of industry trends, competitor offerings, and customer preferences.

Service providers must stay abreast of developments in their respective industries, including emerging technologies, evolving customer demands, and competitive landscapes, to effectively position their products and services in the market. By continuously updating their knowledge base and adapting to changing market dynamics, service providers can offer informed insights, anticipate customer needs, and deliver value-added solutions that enhance the overall customer experience. Ultimately, product and service knowledge serve as foundational pillars for delivering exceptional customer service, fostering customer satisfaction, and driving business growth.

Ineffective communication due to lack of confidence or clarity can hinder customer satisfaction and impede sales efforts. Product and service knowledge play a pivotal role in delivering excellent customer service for several reasons:

Building Trust: When customers interact with knowledgeable service providers who understand the ins and outs of the products or services they offer, it instils confidence and trust. Customers feel reassured knowing that the person assisting them is well-informed and capable of addressing their needs competently.

Providing Accurate Information: A thorough understanding of products and services enables customer service representatives to provide accurate and relevant information to customers. This ensures that customers receive reliable guidance and assistance, leading to informed purchasing decisions and overall satisfaction.

Problem-Solving Abilities: Inevitably, customers may encounter issues or have questions related to the products or services they've purchased. Service providers with comprehensive product knowledge are better equipped to troubleshoot problems effectively, offer solutions, and provide prompt assistance, thereby enhancing the customer experience.

Upselling and Cross-Selling Opportunities: Knowledgeable staff can identify opportunities to recommend complementary products or services based on a customer's needs and preferences. By showcasing additional offerings that align with the customer's interests, service providers can enhance the value of the customer's purchase and potentially increase sales.

Personalised Service: Understanding the intricacies of products and services allows service providers to tailor their assistance to meet the unique needs and preferences of each customer. Whether it's recommending specific features or customising solutions, personalised service fosters a deeper connection with customers and enhances their overall experience.

Handling Objections: Customers may raise objections or express concerns during the purchasing process. Service providers armed with product knowledge can address objections confidently, providing relevant information and overcoming customer hesitations effectively.

As it is so important to develop great product and service knowledge, its helpful to know how to go about it. Here are eight ideas you can try out to enhance your product and service knowledge:

Training Programs: Many companies offer training programs specifically designed to educate employees about their products and services. Take advantage of these opportunities to learn about the features, benefits, and specifications of each offering.

Hands-On Experience: Actively engage with the products or services you're promoting or supporting. Use them yourself, if possible, to gain first-hand experience and better understand their functionality, usability, and potential issues.

Shadowing Co-workers: Shadowing experienced colleagues who excel in product knowledge can provide valuable insights. Observe how they interact with customers, answer inquiries, and address concerns, and ask questions to deepen your understanding.

Study Materials: Utilise product manuals, guides, brochures, and other resources provided by your company to familiarise yourself with key product information. Take the time to read through these materials thoroughly and refer to them as needed.

Online Resources: Explore online resources such as company websites, forums, blogs, and industry publications to stay updated on product developments, trends, and best practices. These sources can offer valuable insights and additional information beyond what's provided internally.

Role-Playing: Practice scenarios where you have to demonstrate your product knowledge, either through role-playing exercises with colleagues or by simulating customer interactions. This can help you refine your communication skills and build confidence in articulating product features and benefits.

Continuous Learning: Commit to ongoing learning and professional development to stay abreast of updates, enhancements, and changes to your company's products and services. Attend workshops, seminars, and webinars, and seek out certification programs relevant to your industry or area of expertise.

Customer Feedback: Pay attention to customer feedback, inquiries, and complaints to identify common issues or areas where additional product knowledge may be needed. Use this feedback as an opportunity to deepen your understanding and improve your ability to assist customers effectively.

By employing these strategies consistently, you can develop a strong foundation of product and service knowledge that will enable you to deliver exceptional customer service and enhance the overall customer experience.

Training and Coaching

As you have now read, to achieve high levels of customer service, success is not merely about pleasant greetings and smiling faces. It involves a complex interplay of skills, knowledge, and a deep commitment to meeting customer needs. Organisations must prioritise the development and support of their frontline staff to ensure consistently exceptional customer experiences.

Customer service training serves as the cornerstone upon which frontline staff build their understanding of the organisation's values, service standards, and customer expectations. Through comprehensive training programs, staff gain essential skills such as active listening, problem-solving, empathy, and effective communication. These programs prepare them to handle diverse scenarios and customer interactions with confidence and professionalism.

Training on specific skill sets can be extremely useful and cut down time and customer complaints. However, training is not a one-time event; it's an ongoing journey. Regular coaching sessions provide personalised guidance and support to frontline staff, helping them refine their customer service skills and address specific challenges. Managers play a crucial role in observing staff interactions, providing constructive feedback, and offering practical tips for improvement. Coaching fosters a culture of continuous learning and growth, empowering staff to take ownership of their development and strive for excellence in every customer interaction. Managers can hone their own skills on leading a team or coaching through their own development and resources like books by the author can help. "Leading a Team", "Practical Leadership" Coaching and Feedback Made Easy" are all designed to help develop these coaching and leadership skills.

The benefits of effective training and coaching extend far beyond individual skill development. Well-trained and coached frontline staff are better equipped to engage with customers proactively, anticipate their needs, and deliver personalised solutions. They feel supported and valued, which translates into increased motivation to exceed customer expectations. Consistent delivery of exceptional customer service creates positive word-of-mouth recommendations and enhances the organisation's reputation in the marketplace.

To maximise the impact of training and coaching initiatives, organisations must adopt best practices that align with their customer service goals and values. Tailored training programs, role-playing exercises, and structured coaching frameworks are essential components of a successful approach. Open communication and feedback between managers and staff create a supportive environment for learning and development. Resources like those found at www.learningplanet.tv where companies can access 1-minute videos techniques and 10-minute short videos can act as ongoing refresher training for skills to be enhanced, reminders to be given and application of those skills easily made.

Ultimately, effective training and coaching empower frontline staff to deliver outstanding customer experiences consistently. They play a pivotal role in building customer loyalty, driving revenue growth, and maintaining a competitive edge in the market. By investing in the development and support of their staff, organisations can elevate their customer service excellence and position themselves for long-term success.

Conclusion

Well, I hope you have enjoyed the ideas and strategies in this book. You will have noticed several recurring themes. In particular, the skills of Active Listening, Being Empathetic and Anticipating Future Needs came up regularly. As a result, I hope they have stood out firmly as key aspects of developing an excellent customer service experience and culture.

Repetition is a way of learning. It's a way of developing. Consider what someone does at the gym. It's repetitive work that builds muscle, stamina and endurance. Likewise, building skills and effectiveness in customer service requires repetition of the traits that customers want and need to be satisfied and return again and again.

Much of these ideas are common sense. They are simple strategies that don't require expensive programs, equipment or higher education. Listen to your customers, show them you truly care and provide an experience for them that shows you value them, their custom and that you want them to keep coming back. If it's not you engaging with customers but people you manage or hire – then ensure you help them develop the same philosophies or you may just be helping your customers 'never come back' and be fuelling your competitors.

References:

You're your customers informed study:

www.1stfinancialtraining.com/Newsletters/trainerstool

kit1Q2009.pdf

Calming Upset customers- Sorry, Glad Sure:

www.mgilearning.com

Moments of Truth by Jan Carlzon published February

15, 1989, by Harper Business

Fish! Philosophy: https://fishphilosophy.com/

Other books available from Derek Good

Coaching and Feedback Made Easy

Kindle and Paperback: 82 pages

First Published: December 23, 2010

ISBN-10: 1453844384

ISBN-13: 978-1453844380

Leading a Team

Kindle and Paperback: 104 pages

First published: August 8, 2012

ISBN-10: 1478332034

ISBN-13: 978-1478332039

Practical Leadership

Kindle and Paperback:

First published: July 4, 2015

ISBN-10: 1512311650

ISBN-13: 978-1512311655

101 Training Activities and How to Run Them

Kindle and Paperback: 254 pages

First published: August 20, 2018

ISBN-10: 1987708784

ISBN-13: 978-1987708783

About the Author

Derek Good's journey from his roots in England to his current residence in the vibrant landscapes of New Zealand is a testament to his unwavering commitment to service excellence. From his early days navigating the world of sales to his role as a works manager in a bustling manufacturing company, Derek's passion for delivering unparalleled service to customers has always been at the forefront of his career.

Driven by a persistent desire to assist customers, Derek's dedication led to the opportunity to lead a company in New Zealand focused on cultivating programs to train others in the field of exceptional customer service. Derek seized it with gusto, viewing it as a chance to wholeheartedly dedicate himself to empowering individuals to excel in serving others.

In 2002, under Derek's leadership, his team clinched the prestigious "Excellence in Service Delivery Award", a testament to the living, breathing embodiment of the principles they imparted to others. Since then, Derek has continued to blaze trails in the realm of service excellence, crafting innovative training programs and penning insightful books aimed at nurturing leadership skills and instilling a steadfast commitment to unparalleled service, regardless of one's role.

Through his remarkable journey, Derek Good has emerged as a beacon of inspiration, empowering individuals and organisations alike to strive for nothing less than service excellence in every endeavour.

Pic: Derek receiving the Excellence in Service Delivery Award 2002

Notes

www.ingramcontent.com/pod-product-compliance
Lightning Source LLC
Chambersburg PA
CBHW071928210526
45479CB00002B/602